1919

Eve L. Ewing

Haymarket Books
Chicago, Illinois

to all those who speak of rivers

to all those who made safe passage and to all those lost in the waters

Published in 2019 by
Haymarket Books
P.O. Box 180165
Chicago, IL 60618
773-583-7884
www.haymarketbooks.org
info@haymarketbooks.org

ISBN: 978-1-60846-602-3

Distributed to the trade in the US through Consortium Book Sales and Distribution (www.cbsd.com) and internationally through Ingram Publisher Services International (www.ingramcontent.com).

This book was published with the generous support of Lannan Foundation and Wallace Action Fund.

Cover artwork by Brian Dovie Golden, www.briandoviegolden.com.
Cover and text design by Rachel Cohen.

Library of Congress Cataloging-in-Publication data is available.

10 9 8 7 6 5 4 3 2

The report contains recommendations, which, if acted upon, will make impossible,
in my opinion, a repetition of the appalling tragedy which brought disgrace to Chicago
in July of 1919.
(*The Negro in Chicago*, xiv)

And she called his name Moses: and she said, Because I drew him out of the water.
(Exodus, Chapter 2, Verse 10, King James Version)

Contents

This book is a story.   3

Before

Exodus 1   8
The Train Speaks   10
in November   12
At the Summit   13
Coming from the Stock Yards   15
keeping house   17
Anatomy: A Treatise on the Manifest Differences of the Negro   20
True Stories About the Great Fire   21

What Happened

Exodus 5   27
or does it explode   30
Jump / Rope   32
The Pearl Diver   34
James Crawford Speaks   35
City in a Garden   37

The Street-Car Speaks   40

sightseers   41

this is a map   43

there is no poem for this   45

Barricade   46

upon seeing a picture of a car in a school book   49

Haibun for July 30   50

After

Exodus 10   54

it wouldn't take much   56

Countless Schemes   59

April 5, 1968   61

July, July!   63

The Day of Undoing   65

I saw Emmett Till this week at the grocery store   68

Acknowledgments   71

Endnotes   73

Photo credits   74

This book is a story.

When I was doing the research that would eventually go into my second book, *Ghosts in the Schoolyard: Racism and School Closings on Chicago's South Side*, and I was writing about segregation in Chicago, one of the most helpful documents I encountered was a report from 1922 called *The Negro in Chicago: A Study on Race Relations and a Race Riot.* Just the title alone enticed me; it was so direct and made such a bold claim on totality. How could someone claim to tell the story of Black people in this city? The whole story? This report was prepared by a committee appointed by the governor, made up of six Black men and six White men, all deemed by their peers to be upstanding and respectable citizens. Its stated purpose was to dissect the 1919 race riot that had happened in Chicago three years prior, to analyze its causes, and try to prevent something like that from happening again. In order to figure out the race riot, the authors reasoned, what they really had to figure out was the reality of everyday life for Black people in their era, and so that's what they set out to do.

For my writing of *Ghosts*, I needed one specific thing from *The Negro in Chicago*, and that was information about housing segregation at the beginning of the Great Migration. But as I was doing my research, I kept getting sucked into other parts of the report, things that were tangential to my work but were so fascinating. They gave me a view into Black life in my city a century earlier, and so many things struck me as being either radically different or completely unchanged. And even though this was a government-commissioned report, many of its passages immediately made me think about poetry. They were so narrative, so evocative, so imagistic. The report was like an old tapestry with loose threads sticking out, and I wanted to tug on them and see what I could unravel, see what new thing I could weave.

And then, there was the matter of the race riot itself. I knew that 1919 had been known as the Red Summer for the wave of race riots that swept across the United States. But, like many aspects of Black history, this was something I didn't learn much about in school, and only then when I was very far along in my academic career. Most of what I knew about 1919, I learned through self-study when I was in graduate school. As a lifelong Chicagoan, I didn't often hear people discuss the race riot that had occurred in our city a century ago, and I wasn't sure that most people knew about it. Chicagoans tend to be enthusiastic and vocal discussants of our own history. But 1919 didn't seem to make it into the timeline alongside titanic stories about Fort Dearborn, Jean-Baptiste Point du Sable, the World's Columbian Exposition, the 1968 riots, Richard J. Daley, or Harold Washington.

This collection of poems is meant as a small offering, an entry point into a conversation about a part of our history that I think is worth talking about much more than we do. Almost every poem in this collection is in conversation with a passage from *The Negro in Chicago*. You'll see those passages written in italics at the top of the page. The page number in parentheses represents the place where you can find the passage in *The Negro in Chicago*. The report is a publicly available document.

I like to use poems as what-if machines and as time-traveling devices, and I'm grateful to have had the chance to do that with this project. I learned a lot, and I hope you learn something too and then go tell someone else about it.

Before

In the beginning of the twentieth century, the first Great Migration was underway. Black people fled the South in droves. They sought an escape from sharecropping and the terror of lynch mobs that tormented innocents. They sought work and better lives for their children. They got on the train and found new homes. Fifty thousand Black people came from the South to Chicago between 1910 and 1920.[1] Many of them were lured by the promises made in the *Chicago Defender*, the Black-owned newspaper that urged them northward on the train. Life in the big city was different than in Mississippi or Alabama. But it brought its own difficulties, including the reality of Northern segregation, overcrowded and substandard housing, the challenge of finding work for fair pay, and the struggle to survive in a harsh new place.

Exodus 1

The stimuli of suggestion and hysteria gave the migration an almost religious significance, and it became a mass movement. . . . Songs and poems of the period characterized the migration as the "Flight Out of Egypt," "Bound for the Promised Land," "Going into Canaan," "The Escape from Slavery," etc. (86)

Now these are the names of the people of Adeline, which came into Mississippi:
Margaret, Prince, Julia, Cora, Amy, Fanny, Celia, and Mollie;
Euginia, Pearlie, Ida, Harper, Vally, and Rosa;
Monroe, Stella, Rogers, Mabeline, Timeus, and Early.
And their people were fruitful and increased abundantly and multiplied,
and their souls were mighty, and the land was filled with them.
And in that land there were many kings, and great store cities to fill with cotton.
And they put planters over the people, and overseers, and made the people tenants,
and the people worked the land. But God was kind to the people,
and the more the people were burdened to work the land, the more they multiplied and spread;
so the planters began to dread the people and worked them ruthlessly.
And the kings held counsel. "Behold," they said,
"the people are more and mightier than we: Come,
let us deal wisely with them; lest they multiply, and it come to pass
that they fight against us, and so get them up out of the land."
And the people, so burdened, held counsel, and they said,
"The lord our God smiles upon us. Why do we stay in the land of these kings?
Come: every son that is born we shall cast into the river,
and every daughter that is born we shall cast into the river."

And the midwives made an ark of leaves and tar, and put the children therein,
and lay them in the waters. And the people gathered at the bank and bade them farewell,
and the river carried them far from the cotton, and the kings and their storehouses of browning blood.

The Train Speaks

. . . the presence of Negroes in large numbers in our great cities is not a menace in itself. (xiii)

Even now, I dream of them,
Quiet nights in the railyard,
When the little rat feet skitter beneath me,
When the last of the strong men with his
gleaming silver buttons has locked the door
and laid his hands against me.
I see them dancing in every passing cloud.

My babies, my babies. Born unto me
in the hills and green lands, loose threads
catching in my sharp parts when they don't watch out,
blistered hands hauling parcels of burlap
as hefty and shapeless as bound cotton.
They move like rabbits, then. They look
for a lash that isn't there, even them that never felt it.
It's in their shoulders. The lash lives in their shoulders.

Long after the last biscuit is gone,
when the sunrise brings steel mountains,
my children look and look through the space
I have made for them, the gift I have prepared.
They are safe within but can see without.

They feel it before they know the words,
then smile when it comes to them—it's flat.
The land is flat. And they smile to think of it,
this new place, the uncle or cousin who will
greet them, the hat they will buy, the ribbons.
They know not the cold, my babies.
They know not the men who are waiting
and angry. They know not that the absence
of signs does not portend the absence of danger.
My children. My precious ones.
I can never take you home. You have none.
And so you go, out into the wind.

in November

FROZEN DEATH BETTER: To die from the bite of frost is far more glorious than that of the mob. I beg of you, my brothers, to leave that benighted land. You are free men.
                    (from the *Chicago Defender*, 88)

the first night I thought / of my last night at home / of my uncle / like a fish / on a line, mouth moving / without speech / eyes like glass / shiny and dead / strung up / on a tree they don't have / here / where the winter / they told me / is death itself / petrified men found / on dirt frozen / to rock / and maybe that will be me / a stone man / a tower of ash / needles where fingers were / and my eyes / too / gone to glass / found here / this first night / beneath a tree / i have never seen / other men weeping in the dark / hearts broken at their belief / that leaving the darkness / meant finding the sun / but in the morning i rise / resurrected, an angel / of the hard black ground

At the Summit

. . . [T]he great opportunity had come to escape from what they felt to be a land of discrimination and subserviency to places where they could expect fair treatment and equal rights. Chicago became to the southern Negro the "top of the world." (2)

By the time they got there, most of the intrepid team had perished. The ground was too hard to bury their bodies. Those that survived laid them in a neat row beneath a cliff overhang and decorated them how they could: a smooth stone here, a bird's feather carried from below, a shining coin from the recesses of a pack. They said words that sounded nice. Holding hands would mean exposure and that would be the end, but each was able to lay a heavy, guarded, enshrouded palm on the shoulder of the next.

And when they arrived at the top of the world at last
 —when all creation was laid before them, the furious wind in their eyes, the possibility
  of descent uncertain—

this was the first thought, a small bloom in each heart. Not the glory that awaited them if they made it back. Not the miracle of this murderous planet. Each thought of the weight of a hand on a shoulder. The heaviness, and the little heat.

Coming from the Stock Yards

The change of home carried with it in many cases a change of status. The leader in a small southern community, when he came to Chicago, was immediately absorbed into the struggling mass of unnoticed workers. School teachers, male and female, whose positions in the South carried considerable prestige, had to go to work in factories and plants because the disparity in educational standards would not permit continuance of their profession in Chicago. (95)

any time I get on the streetcar with the blood of the steers
blossoming across the front of my canvas pants, my clothes call
cattle more than man. not all the white men cringe,
dressed as some are in the same rusting dullness and dread.
every one of us a hook, a slicing knife, a chain, a pile of offal.

forty dollars a week is worth the stain of death, and the smell.
good men make more, or less, by whim. each one of us a foundry.
hands to cut, to carry. knees to bend. this is still new to me.
I called myself a scholar in Georgia, though that was part fancy.
just enough reading and writing to be of worth to my neighbors:

katydid people, summer-song folk. they sent me the children after harvest.
loveliest were the days when we made the woods a grand schoolhouse,
marching two-by-two to the creek to recite Wheatley or Dunbar.
naturalists, the lot of them, calling out every tree by name. every fish.
on the streetcar, I am lonely for them. here, a white boy catches my glance,

pulling his mother's sleeve and whispering loudly. *what's he got?* the
question hangs ugly until I break its hold. I wave the book at him.
read this yet? his eyes drift over the red and the yellow and brown of me.
smiling, he nods. his mother frowns, drawing him nearer. he speaks:
that's tarzan of the apes. my papa read it to me. he told me tarzan is like—

under his mother's coat, he goes on, but his mouth is covered,
voice muffled, and she looks out the window, away from me.
what a thing: to be an invisible man, seen only by a babe. I recall my old pupils:

X is how they signed their names when they first came to me. to each I said *no,*
you have a name, and I wrote with them until they wrote alone,
zoetrope children, moving always and never. zephyr children, wind of my heart.

keeping house

White persons are generally uninformed on matters affecting Negroes and race relations. . . . This same ignorance applies to Negroes, though not to the same degree; for they know white people in their intimate personal and home relations and in connection with their work in factories and stores. They read their books and papers and often hear their discussions. (436)

'do not steal,' she said
'and you can stay here for months.
years, even.' her mouth
a red line, she never asked
if I wanted to stay there.

*

each room has secrets.
in the parlor, an urn rests
near the windowsill
1905. and beneath:
1917. a psalm.

*

she weeps in the tub.
steam crawls beneath the door and
creeps up the window
as I scrub soot from the wall.
dirt still finds the rich.

*

I waited four months.
and now I do steal. small things.
a porcelain mouse.
a black stone from the garden.
she only checks the cupboard.

*

my mother taught me
to be silent in their homes.
they forget you're there.
this way, you pass as a ghost.
come and go as you please, hushed.

*

I learn much this way:
of the city, its powers.
its promises made.
I scour pots and whisper
my plans as water rushes.

*

after seven months
I begin to steal food, too.
a cup of flour.
a brown egg in my bosom.
she no longer speaks to me.

*

at night, when I wait
in the dim hallway to wash,
I touch the black stone.
I wonder at my fortune—
that something like this is mine.

Anatomy: A Treatise on the Manifest Differences of the Negro

THE PROBLEM: The relation of whites and Negroes in the United States is our most grave and perplexing domestic problem. It involves not only a difference of race—which as to many immigrant races has been happily overcome—but wider and more manifest differences in color and physical features. (xxiii)

a splendid dove

contentment

a glass of water

fresh flowers in a vase

"how lovely you look today"

gently falling maple leaves

errant coin in your pocket

in her sleep, surrounded by family

the certainty of dinner

a feather bed

the high keys on a piano

nutmeg

a common starling

the sorrow song swells

water. glass.

in the meadow, a sermon

the streetcar left her standing there

do not look up

ink on the fingers

in the alley, bereft

learn to eat standing up

too soft is bad for the back

rust on porcelain is nice, in its way

the small boy waited all day for his mother.

and when they finally let her go from the big house

and she made her way up the many wooden stairs

he lay on the floor at the threshold

and she heard his stomach's noise over his breath.

her silk scarf, her one good thing, held to his cheek

as he slept.

True Stories About the Great Fire

. . . the sentiment was expressed that Negro invasion of the district was the worst calamity that had struck the city since the Great Fire. A prominent white real estate man said: "Property owners should be notified to stand together block by block and prevent such invasion." (118–19)

Everything they tell you is wrong.
The Great Fire came here in a pair of worn loafers
eating its last sandwich wrapped in paper
and the Great Fire had a smell like grease and flowers.

The Great Fire did not come to eat up the homes.
The homes lay down at the feet of the Great Fire,
for it was godly, and it glowed.
The Great Fire blessed the rooftops.
The Great Fire danced with the lakeshore.

The Great Fire has an auntie who makes dresses
and the Great Fire wears a red pinafore
and dances in a cake walk.

The Great Fire can only move at right angles.
The Great Fire goes from block to block at night
and kisses stray cats in the moonlight
and the cats catch the Holy Ghost.

The Great Fire sits in the balcony and yells at the picture.
The Great Fire sings in a too-loud voice.
The Great Fire has plans for you.
The Great Fire is going to take your daughter someplace.
The Great Fire has a hoard of gold, like a dragon.

The Great Fire already lives next door
and hides in the daytime.
The Great Fire knows they don't want it here.
The Great Fire is going to burn the city they built
and we will watch from the stone tower
and we will wait for it to finish
and we can wait a long time
and the Fire can too.

What Happened

On July 27, 1919, a race riot erupted in Chicago. With the benefit of hindsight, this unto itself is not surprising. Tensions and violence had been mounting in the weeks and months prior, with Black people being attacked seemingly at random by groups of young White men and boys. An ongoing bombing campaign targeted Black people who sought to move out of the city's segregated "Black Belt" or anyone who assisted them with mortgages or realty services, and riots had taken place in nearby East St. Louis, Illinois, on May 28 and July 2. Still, the July 27 riot was devastating in its impact. Twenty-three Black people were killed, fifteen White people were killed, 537 people were injured, 1,000 were made homeless by attacks and arson, and between 5,000 and 6,000 members of the Illinois National Guard were deployed. Most of the violence ended by July 30, but the troops remained until August 8. Much of the violence was blamed on "athletic clubs," organized street gangs of White youth that had powerful political sponsors. The most notable of these groups was "Ragen's Colts," sponsored by Cook County Commissioner Frank Ragen.

The riot began when seventeen-year-old Eugene Williams was killed. Williams had been swimming in an area of Lake Michigan tucked between unofficially segregated beaches. While in the water, he drifted into what was considered the "White area" of the beach, where White people were on the shore throwing rocks at approaching Black people. It is unclear whether Williams was struck by a rock and killed, or whether he remained in the water beyond his capability because he was afraid to return to the shore and be attacked, but ultimately, he drowned. Back on the beach, a group of Black people demanded that a police officer arrest the person deemed responsible, and he refused. Within a few hours, the riot had begun.

Exodus 5

Responsibility for many attacks was definitely placed by many witnesses upon the "athletic clubs," including "Ragen's Colts," the "Hamburgers," "Aylwards," "Our Flag," the "Standard," the "Sparklers," and several others. The mobs were made up for the most part of boys between fifteen and twenty-two. (598)

Daley was elected president of the [Hamburg Athletic] club in 1924, at age twenty-two, a post he held for the next fifteen years. . . . Daley always remained secretive about the riots, and declined to respond to direct questions on the subject.

(*American Pharaoh*, Adam Cohen & Elizabeth Taylor)

And afterward the people went to the chambers of the Pharaoh and told him:
"Thus saieth the Lord God, the God of the prairie and the lake,
God of the flatlands and the railroads, God of vice and God of the disciple,
God of the meatpacker and God of the laundress, God of the lost child,
Let my people go, that they may hold a feast unto me in the bungalows."
And Pharaoh said, "Who is the Lord, that I should obey his voice
to let the people go? I know not your God, neither will I set you free.
I am the one Pharaoh upon the land, and it is I who is Lord upon the flatland.
Lord of the bridge and of the port and the canal and the union, and all the streets
which bear their names. Lord of the bootleg and Lord of brass."
And they said unto Pharaoh, "our God hath met with us: let us go, we pray thee,
lest the Lord our God meet you with plague and pestilence, or with the sword."
And the Pharaoh heard them not, and sent them away, calling them idle.
Then the Lord said unto the people, "Now shalt thou see what I will do to Pharaoh."
The Lord came unto Pharaoh in a dream, and spoke to him, saying,

"Pharaoh, you have been wicked and denied my will.
My people came to you as strangers in a strange land, and you denied them
the land of their pilgrimage, and you have kept them in bondage."
Now you will be punished for your cruelty, and for casting upon them anguish of spirit."
And Pharaoh lived many days under the watchful eye of the Lord God,
until a pestilence rose within him, a sour smoke choking him from within
and though he still appeared in the vestige of man, and a cloud moved into his spirit
and within he was no man but a plague, like rot on the silk of corn,
a filth where sugar had been.

or does it explode

July 27 was hot, 96 degrees, or fourteen points above normal. It was the culmination of a series of days with high temperatures around 95 degrees, which meant that nerves were strained. (11)

man it was so hot

          how hot was it

it was so hot
you could cook an egg
on that big forehead of yours

          you a lie

man i tell you it was so hot

          how hot

it was so hot
i dropped a tomato in the lake
and made campbell's soup

          nuh uh

it was so hot
the sun tried to get in the swimming pool
and everybody else had to get out

          boy that's hot

who you tellin
that day was so hot

          how hot

it was so hot

our dreams laid out on the sidewalk
and said 'never mind, we good'

Jump / Rope

On Sunday, July 27, 1919, there was a clash of white people and Negroes at a bathing-beach in Chicago, which resulted in the drowning of a Negro boy. (xv)

Little Eugene Gene Gene
Sweetest I've seen seen seen
His mama told him him
Them white boys mean mean mean

He didn't listen listen listen
To what mama say say say
Went to the lake lake lake
That July day day day

no, it goes like

Little Eugene W
So sorry to trouble you
Rise, Eugene, rise!
Calm your mama's cries!
Just sit up and look around,
Don't let em bury you down

no, it goes like

Down down baby
Down down, the water's tugging
Sweet sweet baby
Don't make me let you go
Swallow swallow grab the sky
Swallow swallow dark
Swallow swallow grab the sky
Swallow swallow dark
Grandma Grandma sick in bed
Call on Jesus cause your baby's

no, it goes like

All dressed in black black black
All dressed in black black black
All dressed in
And he never came back back back

The Pearl Diver

No arrest was made. The tragedy was sensed by the battling crowd and, awed by it, they gathered on the beach. For an hour both whites and Negroes dived for the boy without results. (4)

uses waves to her favor:
    knows when to resist, which is almost never.
holds the warmth in her tender parts:
    the fat on the hips. the breasts.
pushes the darkness aside:
    refusing the tangle of green.
reaches also for soft things:
    sea cucumber. a slug. the arm of a boy.
grasps also at false starts:
    abalone. mussels. a rock with the shape of a tooth.
blinks at every cloud:
    a burst of sand. blood in the water.

James Crawford Speaks

The Negro crowd from the beach gathered at the foot of Twenty-ninth Street. As it became more and more excited, a group of officers was called by the policeman who had been at the beach. James Crawford, a Negro, fired into the group of officers and was himself shot and killed by a Negro policeman who had been sent to help restore order. (5)

I saw the whites of his eyes
before he let go the railroad tie
that kept him almost afloat
almost alive, almost able to walk home,
almost able to lay out first in the sand
and feel the sun, almost able
to face the stones, almost more
than a stone's throw away, almost
hidden from this terrible place
and its everywhere eyes,
almost free, almost not having
his name in the mouths of fiends,
almost not having his name in my mouth,
almost nobody, nowhere, gone home
to nothing. Me, too. Almost nobody
like me, too. I didn't want to be
somebody, but he was somebody,
because I saw the whites of his eyes

before he let go of the railroad tie.
So I spoke it, his name came out of me,
and I fired.

City in a Garden

after Carl Sandburg

The Negro crowd from Twenty-ninth Street got into action, and white men who came in contact with it were beaten. . . Farther to the west, as darkness came on, white gangsters became active. Negroes in white districts suffered severely at their hands. From 9:00 p.m. until 3:00 a.m. twenty-seven Negroes were beaten, seven were stabbed, and four were shot. (5)

o my ugly homestead,
blood-sodden prairie.

     urbs in horto. meaning:
              if it grows, it once came from dirt

o my love, why do you till the ground with iron?
o my miracle, why do you fire in the dark?
you, thief of dusk. you, captain of my sorrows. you, avarice.
your ground is greedy for our children, and you take them as you please.
the babies come from you, the train car orators, and the beloved hustlers.
they die. and then you send forth more. you, who makes a place
in a middle land. you, ruthless. you, seed ground.
you bear the best of us and the worst in equal measure.

o my garden, which am I?

The Street-Car Speaks

Street-car routes, especially transfer points, were thronged with white people of all ages. Negro passengers were dragged to the street, beaten, and kicked. (6)

not this freedom. I / lost them, my wires sparking / amidst the bruises.

sightseers

Often the "sightseers" and even those included in the nucleus did not know why they had taken part in crimes the viciousness of which was not apparent to them until afterward. (23)

"The sad truth is that most evil is done by people who never make up their minds to be good or evil."
(Hannah Arendt, *The Life of the Mind*)

just this once I hope you'll forgive me
for writing a somewhat didactic poem
I just didn't know how else to say
that we live in a time of sightseers
standing on the bridge of history
watching the water go by
and there are bodies in the water
and the water has been dirty for so long
and the sightseers still drink from it
they buy special filters and they smile
they have nice glasses and teacups
they put sugar in the dirty water
that has our bodies in it

and there are sightseers
seated beneath the tower of empire
peering up at the lights

and there are children in the tower
and the tower has been crooked for so long
and the sightseers still look at it
they find the lights enchanting
they meet up on the weekends
they have picnics in the plaza of the tower
that has our children in it

and there are sightseers
looking at the house of power
waiting to take a tour
and there are devils in the house
and the house has been wicked for so long
and the sightseers still worship it
they stand in front and take pictures
they marvel at the white pillars
they send postcards of the house
that has the devils in it

and just this once I hope you'll forgive me
for asking you directly
to forget the lovely water
to forget the charming pillars
because there are children in the tower
there are children in the tower
there are children in the tower
and they are dead already

this is a map

Samuel Bass, on account of the street-car strike, was walking the five and one-half miles from his work to his home when a gang of white men knocked him down three times, and cut gashes in his nose and cheeks with their shoes. Bass hid behind freight cars till a Jewish peddler took him in his cart to State Street. A doctor was visited, but when he learned that Bass had no money, he turned him away without treatment. (659)

this is a map of my city
here are the places in my city where I dare not go
here is where the electric wires gave out and here
is where I still had to make it home,
and here is the first mile, where I whistled
the way my granny taught me, to keep away the haints
and here is where a baby waved to me from a window
and here is the second mile, where I heard the calls,
and on this map there is no third mile
in this, my city, where I first prayed to die,
and then, hearing a single cardinal over the din of their threats,
changed my mind, and prayed to live,
and this is a map of my neighbor's city
where he traces a way through the mud each day,
the squeal of old wood on iron heralding his arrival,
a king of the streets, a conquering hero of nowhere, and
this is a map of my body

this is the blood of my rivers
this is the bruise of my marshland
this is the sinew of my furthest ridge, and
this is a map of the railroad.
and if I could stand and walk I could make it all the way back
to my granny, pinching snuff and humming
and if she looked up she would say *boy, my baby*
where you been all this time

there is no poem for this

A mob of white civilians, soldiers, and sailors, who had been chasing Negroes through the "Loop" district for the previous two or three hours, beating and robbing them, and destroying property where Negroes were not found, entered one of Thompson's restaurants where Hard-wick was breakfasting. Another Negro, one King, was also in the restaurant. The mob set upon them, throwing food and dishes. Hardwick dodged into the street and King hid behind a dish counter, where he was wounded with a knife. Failing to catch Hardwick as he fled down Adams Street, one of the rioters stepped to the curb and fired a revolver at him, bringing him down. Several of the crowd robbed the corpse. (666)

Barricade

"'Sniping' was a form of retaliation by Negroes which grew out of the automobile raids. These raiding automobiles were fired upon from yards, porches, and windows throughout the 'Black Belt.' One of the most serious cases reported was at Thirty-first and State streets, where Negroes barricaded the streets with rubbish boxes." (18)

my father told me to get the refuse in the street and not be too proud to touch it with my hands

i   the
never   smell
heard   was
a   not
roar   the
like   worst
that   thing
in   the
all   fear
my   was
days   like
before   choking
or since   on air

i mean the motorcycle   when it barreled toward me   like a dart   and i just stood
watching the gleaming metal   and also i mean the man's cry
when he fell   and also i mean   the roar of my father
when he shot the man down   and also i mean the engine
that just kept going
though its master lay dying
in the trash heap

upon seeing a picture of a car in a school book

Automobile raids were added to the rioting Monday night. Cars from which rifle and revolver shots were fired were driven at great speed through sections inhabited by Negroes. Negroes defended themselves by "sniping" and volley-firing from ambush and barricade. So great was the fear of these raiding parties that the Negroes distrusted all motor vehicles. (6)

one hundred years ago, before the Burning Days,
they rode in metal carriages, grandma says.
rich people did. big iron capsules on fat rubber wheels.
like a buggy, but with no horses. no one to talk to
or feed. I asked her "well what is a driver if no living being
is the one driven? what is a tire if no one has to
breathe to make it work?" and she laughs right at me.
the autos took their roar from a vapor, drawn from the ground.
an ancient something. something that could run out.
I asked her "well what does it mean to move on earth
through the will of something with no heart inside?
well what would you do if you had more than four friends?"
they gave up the heavy vessels when we built our city.
we live as we should, now, moving in good things that let us
touch the ground and feel the shape of the earth.
bicycles and wheelchairs. ponies and roller skates.
when I greet my Lavender with her water and hay, I say,
"good morning, and who could ever want you to be anything
but just as you are? just as god made you—on your own feet?"
and she says the same back to me.

Haibun for July 30

Rain on Wednesday night and Thursday drove idle people of both races into their homes. The temperature fell, and with it the white heat of the riot. (7)

Sparrows in the elms fluffed and shook until they looked like eggs again, fat brown feathered eggs, hidden amid the boughs and crowded against one another. Just so, they curled each toe over the givingness of the narrow wood, just so, as their ancestors had in a place across the ocean. They had never seen the ocean, but tonight they knew water again. Just so, they knew the right corner, the right way to lean, the right way to be to nestle just beneath a canopy of leaves. Enough to live for now beneath the green but still watch it all come down before closing eyes to sleep. The tip of one branch, the place where its strength gave in to the most delicate almost-nothing, gave way to its last leaf. Its tender ribs held the rain until they could not, and it bowed and sprang back and bowed and sprang back, drop by drop. And with every small pool that it let go, the rivulets cascading over a stone cornice grew stronger, spilling in their turn down to the street. Someone watches from within, relieved to open the curtains just enough to see the elm-dwellers in their old, sodden city.

after days of blood,
candles in the window again.
birds shake off the rain.

After

In nine of the thirty-eight deaths resulting from the riot, a grand jury indicted an individual on a murder charge, and four of those individuals were convicted— two White and two Black. No one was convicted for the death of Eugene Williams. Daniel Callahan, the police officer who refused to make an immediate arrest, was dismissed from the police force and then later reinstated.

The riot left an indelible mark on the city: its sense of boundaries, of relationships between neighbors, of fear and mistrust were cemented for a century to come.

Exodus 10

There is nothing in the make-up of a Negro, physically or mentally, which should induce anyone to welcome him as a neighbor. The best of them are insanitary, insurance companies class them as poor risks, ruin alone follows in their path.
(from a 1920 issue of the *Property Owners' Journal*, 151)

And the Lord said unto the people,
"Stretch out thy hands toward heaven,
that there may be darkness over the city,
even darkness which may be felt."
And the people stretched forth their hands,
and there was a thick darkness in all the city:
it weighed heavy on the heads of saint
and sinner alike. And the people smiled upon the darkness,
and the darkness was good. For upon them the darkness
was as burnt sugar: pleasing to the skin, and sweet upon the lips.
And the people delighted in the darkness.
But upon the wicked, the darkness was as a plague,
and beneath it they writhed in torment, weeping and calling for mercy.
The thickness of the darkness was such that they saw not one another,
neither rose any from their place for days. And the people found leisure,
calling to one another through the darkness as in a child's game,
and they found each other in laughter. And to them, all noise was joyful
in the darkness, so that each found the work of the Lord
in the song of the sparrow or the sigh of a sleeping infant. And it was good.

But the wicked people were slothful, and found only misery in their repose.
And the kings, their hearts hardened, called unto the people, and said,
"Go! Get thee from us! Take heed to thyselves, and leave the city."
But the people stood in the darkness, and each reached with a staff
toward heaven, and they spoke as one, saying then "Nay,
for the Lord our God is with us, and the city is granted unto us,
and it shall be a city of darkness for all days to come."

it wouldn't take much

[Officer Callahan] gave his racial philosophy freely in the following remarks: . . . It wouldn't take much to start another riot, and most of the white people of this district are resolved to make a clean-up this time. (451)

We have been informed that the City's ████████████████ will activate when the ████
██
████████████████████████ public ████████████████████████████████████
██
████████ expect[s] ██
████ unrest. ████████████

rest[.] ██
██
████████████████████████████████████

a decision ████████████████ a verdict ████████████ Sunday

██
██
██
████████████ if civil unrest becomes ████████████████████████ your home, please
always remember ████████████████ [the] night.

███ any mob[,] ██████████
██ a████████ police immediate████████████████████

████████████████████████████████ do not let anyone follow[.] ███████████████
████████████████████████████████████ Stay[.] █████████████████

your best friend before and during a crisis ████████████████ Stay[.] ████████████
████████████████████████████ Know where the danger ██████████████████
████████████████ hits its peak.

While a crisis is ████████████your ████████████radio[,] ██████████████████
██ resources █████████████
will be █ tremendous ████████████████

Since there's a good chance you will be confined to your home ████████████ you will want
to make sure you have enough ██
████████████████████████████ home.

Home is generally the safest place to be during ████████████████████ riots[.]

████████████████ don't go out[.] ██████████

look. The last thing you want is ████████████ the chaos.

However, should you find yourself outside ██████████████████████ stay away

████████████████████ make your ████████home ████████possible.

██ on a day to day level, ██
██████████████████████████████ your wits ██████████ your eyes ██████████████ means
█████████ getting out ████████████████████████

Keep ██ focus[.] ████████
█████████████████████████ Keep your focus on the present

██ what is happening ██████████████████████████ before it escalates █████████
█████████████ be █████████ safe!

an erasure of the email I received from the management of my apartment building the day of the Jason Van Dyke verdict, October 2018.

Countless Schemes

Countless schemes have been proposed for solving or dismissing this problem, most of them impracticable or impossible. Of this class are such proposals as: (1) the deportation of 12,000,000 Negroes to Africa; (2) the establishment of a separate Negro state in the United States; (3) complete separation and segregation from the whites and the establishment of a caste system or peasant class; and (4) hope for a solution through the dying out of the Negro race. (xxiii)

1
you don't have enough boats

we came here head to toe
and now we are millions
and now we demand to sit upright

and so you don't have enough boats

2
you would give us the most wretched desert,
not the desert of our fathers where God is watching
and manna comes down like the snow.
you would give us all that is barren
you would give our children sand to eat

3
we been had that

4

you said
hope for a solution through the dying out of the Negro race
hope for a solution through the dying out of the Negro
hope for a solution through the dying out

you said hope for the Negro dying
hope through the dying
hope for the dying out
the solution dying

you said dying. the Negro
the Negro dying
the Negro hope
hope the Negro

you said hope for dying
hope dying
dying
dying

you said hope

April 5, 1968

after Gwendolyn Brooks

Our country is over, you see. Here lies
my prettiest baby, and her glass fingertips are
all over the tar. In the before I told
her, 'play, beloved,' and
from the storefront piano came legends
of the mountaintop and it made
me weep. I was an ugly phoenix
but our dirt was our own. As the sun rises
now I know what we do is right. Unafraid
I stand before the skinny boy with the
bayonet & say 'before I'll be an ashen ghost, black
gone gray at your hand like our dead philosopher,
I'll burn my own, you see, just the way I want, & you will
know it's mine.' Goodbye, Madison. I will remember
my country, my sun-up town. Because there
on the mountaintop I saw the fire in the valley. They
were coming to take you away. They came
with cursed water, the hurting river they used to
strike down the children of Birmingham, each life
a bad joke in their bull eyes. And
I said 'not here. Not never. Not Madison.' And exulted
in the shadow of the first fire, then the next, the

heat sending sweat into my eyes, that simple salt hurt

keeping me from thinking too long of your piano gone mute.

I suspect the boy wanted to run then

but he stood shaking, gun raised, and I said, 'if this is it,

if this is my last day that ever was,

man, at least I know I got over,

that the likes of you will never have us, that the

street I call my only home burned to dust

at my hand. Let them sing of how bright the sun was as

a coward struck me down. They

will tell it always, they will say

that one glorious morning, I showed them your heart, lest they think it was settled.'

July, July!

in remembrance of the 739 people who lost their lives that week in 1995.

one summer in Chicago the people baked to death in brick,
mouths open for water or to say *my lord*
or to say *I love you mama* or to sing
or their eyes closed and they died in their sleep,
sweat spelling the shape of an angel against floral patterns
spilling into the quilted stitching a new map:
not just one river but many, tracing an X and an X and another
full of salt water like the coasts we never met.
that summer or maybe it was
the summer before or
another summer or
every summer,
we lay on our backs,
the one good comforter protecting us
from the nails and staples in the floorboards
that would have etched their little brands
into our still-baby skin, metal pressing through
my thin cotton undershirt like a toothache
in my pillowcase i hid books and used kleenex.
each night i listened to my brother wheeze.
i prayed for rain to come.
i said *i love you*

i didn't say *it's too hot to breathe right*
i said *goodnight*
i didn't say whether i would give up or not
i said *this is still home*
i said *my lord*

The Day of Undoing

The part near Twenty-seventh Street had by tacit understanding come to be considered as reserved for Negroes, while the whites used the part near Twenty-ninth Street. Walking is not easy along the shore, and each race had kept pretty much to its own part, observing, moreover, an imaginary boundary extending into the water. (4)

All boundaries are conventions, waiting to be transcended. One may transcend any convention if only one can first conceive of doing so.
(*Cloud Atlas*, David Mitchell)

"Every boundary is imaginary," said the wild-haired girl, standing atop the wooden crate. They listened at her feet, rapt. The children had come from all over—lake children and desert children, mountain children, children of the marsh. Many of them had walked hundreds of miles, and walking is not easy—for anyone, but especially for the small. They came carrying baby cousins, and dolls, worn bookbags, and sweaters tied around the waist. They came to hear her and what she had to tell them before tomorrow's real sojourn.

They planned it, in secret, for months. Some of them practiced at night, when the adults were asleep. They rose in the darkness, went out to some quiet place, closed their eyes, and walked. They walked in the way she had taught them: a heel moving in a perfect sweep to meet the toe, the smallest step to ensure the straightest line. They held their arms out like they had maybe seen in the circus or in a book about the circus. Walking is not easy, but they did it, because the sound of her voice was so like a tiny magic, so like something sweet underneath the tongue, so like a friend. When she spoke to them each of them felt the most acute joy, washing over them like a lucid dream. Her speaking was like a mother soothing a wound, or a stray dog being friendly, or the juice of a mango on the chin. It was everything good.

And now, after so much practice, the day was here. Some of them called it, in their different ways of speaking, *the unmaking day*, or *the day of undoing*, or just *the walking day*. Some of the littlest ones called it *walkfly time*. That was their funny baby word for it, but as such words often are—funny baby words—it was perhaps the most truthful.

Now they were here, listening, and it was all really going to happen, and it was all they could do not to jump up and yell in their anticipation. Some of them did just that, and a few others, and soon as she watched over them they were all leaping and hollering, cartwheeling and somersaulting, doing the many dances of their many homes and the little ones just gumming on pieces of bread and watching through toothless grins, and they all danced like that until they were tired and it was time to sleep.

They lay out under the stars, and she wanted them to sleep well, for they would rise with the sun, and so she sang them a song about the lake and the desert and mountain and the marsh, and they slept like that, tangled together under the canopy of her voice.

And when the sun appeared, they all murmured and stood one by one, wiping the sleep from their eyes and stretching their legs, preparing for what was to come next.

And all the grown people came outside, searching, wondering where
their children had gone, calling their names and crying out for them. But
presently they stopped their calling, because there they all were, countless
of them. Countless children, standing firmly front to back, their arms out.
Standing on lines that no one could see, lines in the dirt and the desert and
the lake that no one could see but which for some reason they had treated as
gospel all their lives.

The children stood and they smiled, toes pointed forward the way she
had taught them. And the grown people looked up when they heard the
voice of someone they could not see, but the voice was like something soft,
something they thought they remembered from another time, and they
looked back at the children and the children were walking, but they were
not touching the sand or the rock or the water anymore, they were walking
in the air, one foot before the last, each toe touching each heel, and all
around them there was a light and they were more beautiful than they had
ever looked, and the grown people wept, and the voice said

now

I saw Emmett Till this week at the grocery store

There is no time to be lost. Other matters must be put aside for the moment and a solution reached for Chicago's greatest problem. (44)

looking over the plums, one by one
lifting each to his eyes and
turning it slowly, a little earth,
checking the smooth skin for pockmarks
and rot, or signs of unkind days or people,
then sliding them gently into the plastic.
whistling softly, reaching with a slim, woolen arm
into the cart, he first balanced them over the wire
before realizing the danger of bruising
and lifting them back out, cradling them
in the crook of his elbow until
something harder could take that bottom space.

I knew him from his hat, one of those
fine porkpie numbers they used to sell
on Roosevelt Road. it had lost its feather but
he had carefully folded a dollar bill
and slid it between the ribbon and the felt
and it stood at attention. he wore his money.
upright and strong, he was already to the checkout
by the time I caught up with him. I called out his name

and he spun like a dancer, candy bar in hand,
looked at me quizzically for a moment before
remembering my face. he smiled. *well
hello young lady*

     *hello, so chilly today
     should have worn my warm coat like you*

yes so cool for August in Chicago

     how are things going for you

oh he sighed and put the candy on the belt
it goes, it goes.

Acknowledgments

The poems "Anatomy: A Treatise on the Manifest Differences of the Negro," "Countless Schemes," and "upon seeing a picture of a car in a school book" previously appeared in *The Rumpus*. "April 5, 1968" first appeared in *Chicago Magazine*. "July, July!" first appeared in *Redivider*. "I saw Emmett Till this week at the grocery store" first appeared in *Tin House*. I am grateful to the editorial wizards at each of those publications for kindly offering a home for my work.

Thank you to the phenomenal Danez Smith for their gracious editorial eye on this manuscript. I am always in awe of you, you ceaseless miracle. Thank you to the team at Haymarket Books, who are always exceptionally generous and supportive toward me but were in rare form in the patience and kindness they showed toward this book project. In particular, thank you to the magnificent Julie Fain and Jim Plank, to whom I owe not only gratitude for this project but for much of my literary career, such as it is. Tabia Yapp keeps me busy, keeps me on point, keeps me hopeful, and keeps me eating, and I am always thankful for that. Keenan Smith provided extremely helpful assistance with managing the source text for this book and pored through all my notes and highlights to pull things together out of the muck—thank you.

I read these poems out loud in many places before they made it into this book. If you were in a room with me and gave me the space to do that, to try them out and see how they fit into the world, I appreciate you for that, and I thank you. Thank you to my colleagues at the University of Chicago for your ongoing support, which I do not take for granted.

I have been blessed with love, support, and assistance from innumerable poets, but in particular, thanks to Hanif Abdurraqib, Nate Marshall, and Amanda Torres for their attention along the way with this project, and to Fatimah Asghar for her constant reassurance and encouragement. I would like to say thank you to these poets for many things, but most immediately, just for being as you are:

Elizabeth Acevedo, Kaveh Akbar, Mahogany Browne, Safia Elhillo, Shira Erlichman, Adam Falkner, Jacqui Germain, Terrance Hayes, Sarah Kay, Angel Nafis, Hieu Minh Nguyen, José Olivarez, Morgan Parker, Joseph Rios, Diamond Sharp, Clint Smith, Sofía Snow, Jamila Woods. I am just grateful to live in the era in which you live. I am indebted to the gracious guidance and living example of many, including Tara Betts, Ross Gay, Tyehimba Jess, and Patricia Smith.

Thank you to my marvelous family. Thank you always to my biggest supporter, my teammate, my friend, my beloved, Damon Jones.

Endnotes

1. St. Clair Drake and Horace R. Cayton, *Black Metropolis: A Study of Negro Life in a Northern City* (Chicago: University of Chicago Press, 2015), 58.

Photo credits

p 1   Jun Fujita. *Ogden Cafe during the 1919 Chicago Race Riots*. 1919. Chicago History Museum, Jun Fujita negatives collection: Nitrate negatives, Box 1 of 1 (NN0139).

p 6   Chicago Commission on Race Relations. *A negro family just arrived in Chicago from the rural South*. 1922. Schomburg Center for Research in Black Culture, Jean Blackwell Hutson Research and Reference Division, Shelf locator: Sc 323.173-I.

p 14   Chicago Commission on Race Relations. *Negro stock yards workers receiving wages*, 1922. Schomburg Center for Research in Black Culture, Jean Blackwell Hutson Research and Reference Division, Shelf locator: Sc 323.173-I.

p 23   Jun Fujita. *Crowd during the 1919 Chicago Race Riots*. 1919. Chicago History Museum, Jun Fujita negatives collection: Nitrate negatives, Box 1 of 1 (NN0139).

p 29   Jun Fujita. *National Guard during the 1919 Chicago Race Riots*. 1919. Chicago History Museum, Jun Fujita negatives collection: Nitrate negatives, Box 1 of 1 (NN0139).

p 38–39 Chicago Commission on Race Relations. *Armed crowds searching for a negro*. 1922. Schomburg Center for Research in Black Culture, Jean Blackwell Hutson Research and Reference Division, Shelf locator: Sc 323.173-I.

p 48   Chicago Commission on Race Relations. *Negroes being escorted to safety zones*. 1922. Schomburg Center for Research in Black Culture, Jean Blackwell Hutson Research and Reference Division, Shelf locator: Sc 323.173-I.

p 52–53 Chicago Commission on Race Relations. *Negroes under protection of police leaving wrecked house in riot zone*. 1922. Schomburg Center for Research in Black Culture, Jean Blackwell Hutson Research and Reference Division, Shelf locator: Sc 323.173-I.

p 70   Chicago Commission on Race Relations. *Buying ice from freight car switched into Negro residence area*. 1922. Schomburg Center for Research in Black Culture, Jean Blackwell Hutson Research and Reference Division, Shelf locator: Sc 323.173-I.

About Haymarket Books

Haymarket Books is a radical, independent, nonprofit book publisher based in Chicago.

Our mission is to publish books that contribute to struggles for social and economic justice. We strive to make our books a vibrant and organic part of social movements and the education and development of a critical, engaged, international left.

We take inspiration and courage from our namesakes, the Haymarket martyrs, who gave their lives fighting for a better world. Their 1886 struggle for the eight-hour day—which gave us May Day, the international workers' holiday—reminds workers around the world that ordinary people can organize and struggle for their own liberation. These struggles continue today across the globe—struggles against oppression, exploitation, poverty, and war.

Since our founding in 2001, Haymarket Books has published more than five hundred titles. Radically independent, we seek to drive a wedge into the risk-averse world of corporate book publishing. Our authors include Noam Chomsky, Arundhati Roy, Rebecca Solnit, Angela Y. Davis, Howard Zinn, Amy Goodman, Wallace Shawn, Mike Davis, Winona LaDuke, Ilan Pappé, Richard Wolff, Dave Zirin, Keeanga-Yamahtta Taylor, Nick Turse, Dahr Jamail, David Barsamian, Elizabeth Laird, Amira Hass, Mark Steel, Avi Lewis, Naomi Klein, and Neil Davidson. We are also the trade publishers of the acclaimed Historical Materialism Book Series and of Dispatch Books.

About the Author

Eve L. Ewing is a sociologist and a writer from Chicago. She is an assistant professor at the University of Chicago School of Social Service Administration and the author of *Ghosts in the Schoolyard: Racism and School Closings on Chicago's South Side* and *Electric Arches*. She is the coauthor (with Nate Marshall) of the play *No Blue Memories: The Life of Gwendolyn Brooks* and also writes for Marvel Comics.

CPSIA information can be obtained
at www.ICGtesting.com
Printed in the USA
LVHW041503140519
617473LV00002B/4/P